The Lost Hope of the Hopeless Romantic

C. E. Haas

The Lost Hope of the Hopeless Romantic

ISBN 978-0-6151-5029-1

Based on a true story. Names and certain identifying details have been changed
for privacy reasons.

This book is dedicated to three people:

My mother, for bringing me into this world,

My best friend, for forcing me to make a promise that kept me in it,

And Ingrid, my counselor, for helping me see it in a better light.

"Time doesn't heal all wounds, although it does scab them over fairly well."

Book of Ley

"Some stories begin at the end."

Book of Ley

Journal: Sunday October 22, 2006

Wedding Day

Today is my wedding day. Was my wedding day. Would have been my wedding day. Even now, I still love her and always will.

Journal: Tuesday October 17, 2006

Lost Love

Depression alternates with acceptance. Sometimes a little happiness. My feelings seem to be cyclical. Love lost. New love found. Love lost again.

Journal: Saturday October 7, 2006

Two Women

My heart aches with love for two women, but I'll never again have either. I shared my feelings with a good friend today. She told me the fact that I still love them means my love was real. Guess I really am a hopeless romantic.

I've thought I've loved other women in my life, but I suppose Julie and Gabrielle are the only ones still in my heart because I wasn't mature enough to truly know what love was before them.

Part of me dreams of using some elaborate romantic gesture to win either one of them back. The rest of me knows that part makes me a fool. It's a hopeless cause.

Blog: Friday October 6, 2006

4 Years Ago Today

It's hard not to think about what happened exactly 4 years ago today. A beautiful sunset. A lovely girl. A daring proposal.

With that memory comes a flood of memories from last year. A heart still filled with love for some and hatred for others. A soul gripped with anger.

But the past is over. Pushed to the corner with the hope of forgetting.

"Sometimes we can choose to be happy."

Book of Ley

Happy

It seems like every time I post a blog about things going well, things quickly unravel in the next month or so. Well, I don't think that's going to happen now, so I'm going to take the chance.

Some of you are probably wondering why I'm up so late, since I have to get up for work in a few hours. I was just watching the video my stepfather took at Ed and Beth's wedding. I was able to see a lot of things I missed while handling my best man duties. Some of the things Ed's family had to say brought tears to my eyes. Although I'm sad Ed and Beth will be moving several hours away from here at the end of August, I'm still overwhelming happy that the two of them found happiness with each other and are now enjoying married life and that Ed found a job in his field (even though he is making significantly more than me ☺). I truly could not have better friends. It's just amazing how the happiness of those people who are close to us can infect us (like the flu ☺) and make us happy with them.

Of course, part of my happiness comes from other areas. I love my new job. Working with troubled kids is definitely where I'm supposed to be. I know I'm making a difference. I anticipate many years with this company (and definitely other positions, moving around and up). My goal is to save up for a down payment on a condo in a nice area I have my eye on (after paying down some debt) so I can move back out of my parents' house. Hopefully I can do that in about a year.

Oh, romantically. Things are going very well there as well. I'm not going to kiss and tell, but I'm dating casually and having a great time. Haven't had a bad date since I started dating again several weeks back. I've learned not to push and to just have fun. Whatever happens, happens.

"Like the nectar of the gods, life is oh so sweet."

Book of Ley

One of the Happiest Days of My Life

June 24th was one of the happiest days of my life. I was the best man at the wedding of my two closest friends (who I actually introduced ☺). I was expecting some of my joy to be offset by a few things: my ex-fiancée being one of the bridesmaids, photos being taken exactly where I proposed to my ex, the day being my ex's birthday, etc.

I was pleasantly surprised that I enjoyed the entire day with no reservations. The whole day was wonderful. I cannot begin to describe the joy I felt when two of the people I love most dearly became husband and wife. Seeing the love in their eyes and knowing I helped bring that about meant more to me than words can describe.

Of course, a few other things put the icing on the cake of that happy day, like seeing that my ex was still a little overweight and catching her pointing jealously at me and my beautiful date gliding all over the dance floor. That may sound petty, but those things made me feel pretty good.

In Judaism, there's sort of an old wives' tale that matching three couples who get married gives one an automatic pass into Heaven (even though a Jewish belief in Heaven/Paradise is a relatively recent one). So I just need to make two more matches. ☺

Best Man Speech Excerpts

... Ed and I have known each other for more than a decade, and we've been best friends since high school.

I'm an only child, as is Ed, but sometimes when people ask me if I have any siblings, I tell them I have a best friend who is like a brother. We've shared a lot of good, bad, and interesting memories ...

Normally, the best man is really close to the groom and not so much with the bride. That is not the case today. Beth and I are very good friends. I've actually known Beth a little longer than Ed has. In fact, I'm the one who brought them together. Several years back, we had a game and movie night. I brought Ed. Julie brought Beth. Later, Ed told me he thought Beth was giving him signals, and he wanted to put his arm around her during the movie, but he wasn't sure if he should.

A few days later, I jokingly told Beth that Ed had a crush on her. Her wide-eyed response of "Really?" told me that she was the one with the crush on Ed ...

So for me it is a double honor to be best man today, and I am doubly happy because my two closest friends are now married, and I'm here to share that joy with them ...

Marriage is more than just that piece of paper that says you're now Mr. and Mrs. ... It's a symbol of your commitment to each other and your love for each other and your desire to start your own new family.

Family isn't just the people who are related to you by blood. Family is the group of people you care about. Like I said earlier, Ed, I think of you as a brother. My parents consider you their "second son." Now that you and Beth are married, it's like I'm gaining a sister. Beth, I have to give you a hug. {Hug} Welcome to the family.

In Judaism, there is a phrase that means congratulations/best wishes/good luck. Please raise your glasses, and repeat after me: mazel tov.

Ed and Beth, mazel tov!

And l'chaim! To life!

Journal: Monday June 19, 2006
Things Are Okay

I stuck by my rule and didn't date until May, and even then it was only a blind date to meet the girl I'm taking to Ed and Beth's wedding. No dates since then.

I'm waiting on a call to find out if I got the job working as a youth counselor. A job is the most important piece to the puzzle of putting my life back together.

I have some new friends, so I don't need to worry about that. I'm not really caring about women, either. I'm not looking for anything long-term. Maybe something short-term.

Tomorrow Never Comes

Life fades into memories,
Memories mix with dreams,
The past becomes a jumble,
Only the future still unseen.

The present always here,
Tomorrow never comes.

The past continues growing,
The future forever infinite,
The present one short moment.

Never tomorrow,
Always today.

Movie Plot

Everyone I've shared my story with in the past week has said the same thing: it's like a movie. Only, no one would actually believe it. In four months, I'm going to be the best man at my best friend's wedding. The bride is also a close friend. I actually brought them together. One of the bridesmaids is my ex-fiancée; she's one of the bride's closest friends. The actual date of the wedding? My ex's birthday. Our wedding was going to be this fall, on my best friend's birthday. Where are they going to have the pictures taken? The same place I proposed to my ex, where we were also going to get our wedding pictures done. One of the groomsmen used to be one of my closest friends, until he betrayed me by encouraging my ex to get rid of me while I was working in another state. Not because he wanted her, as he's actually married to another one of the bridesmaids. He didn't think we had a good relationship, so he decided to "help" by breaking us up and saying all kinds of nasty things about me. The wedding would be the climax of a totally unbelievable movie.

Journal: Wednesday February 22, 2006
Wakeup Call

My back hurts, and the bed is hard. In the moment before I fully awake, I wonder where I am. In a sudden rush of mental pain, it all comes back: the lost loves, the lost friends, the way my life fell apart, the suicide plan, checking into the behavioral unit of the hospital. As I swing my legs over the side of the bed, I remember how close I came to not waking up at all today. Had I not decided to try calling the college counseling center just one more time, I would have gone home and followed through with my plan. I am now a "mental patient." Oh, joy. Sigh.

"The strongest steel is forged in the hottest flames."

Book of Ley

Life Sucks

Life is HORRIBLE! A lot of bad things have been going on, but the thing that topped it all off was Gabrielle breaking up with me. Today will be the last day I write in here because I'm going to kill myself. Not just 'cause of Gabrielle. That was just the straw that broke the camel's back. I left instructions for Ed in a sealed envelope on his front door.

My one chance was the counseling center at my grad school. I promised Ed I'd go here before I did anything. I also asked G-d to give me a sign. Well, when I got here, the counseling center was closed and locked. Apparently they don't have classes and some things are closed here the Tuesday after President's Day.

I can't ask for a clearer sign than that.

"Not having one's love returned is like not being able to breathe; it just takes longer to suffocate."

Book of Ley

Suicide Note

To everyone:

I'm really sorry that I hurt you like this, but please know that I'm happier now. I had to do what was best for me.

I'm sure you are all wondering why I did this. I think all of you know I was having a difficult time after Julie and I broke up. When I came back to New Jersey after spending the summer at camp, all my future plans were shattered. I had no job, little money, felt betrayed by a few close friends, and had to move back in with my parents, and there were several other things were going on that some of you were aware of. I could barely handle all the crap in my life. I went on a lot of really bad first dates and was getting really depressed with everything when I started going out with Gabrielle on December 2nd. Things were finally starting to look my way. A few days after my 24th birthday, Gabrielle told me she loved me, and I loved her back, even though it took me awhile to be completely sure. I was briefly happy.

Unfortunately, that happiness was fleeting. My money was rapidly depleting and I had to mostly wipe out my savings, a gas station attendant forgot to put the oil cap back on my car, causing thousands of dollars worth of damage, and several others things were also going on. I felt like I was in a juggling act and almost all of my balls had fallen to the ground. I was barely hanging on. A few weeks ago Gabrielle told me she no longer loved me, but she still cared for me a great deal. She also said she was uncomfortable with our relationship and couldn't give me a reason. I tried to deal with this state of affairs. On Friday, I couldn't fall asleep on her sofa because I was too uncomfortable and felt it was ridiculous to be sleeping in separate rooms after over a month of sleeping in the same bed at each other's houses. I left angry, went home, couldn't go to sleep, and finally talked to Gabrielle online very late that night. She thought I dumped her, but I didn't. She proceeded to break up with me. I've tried to contact her several times to talk, but she won't respond to my emails, IM's, or voicemail messages. I couldn't deal with this as well.

I love Gabrielle, and I still love Julie (even though we were not right for each other). I never fully got over Julie, and the breakup with Gabrielle just got piled on top of that. The only thing that was really going well for me was my workouts; I was actually in the best shape of my life, but it didn't make me feel much better. I have no job, no car, and very little money. I basically only have two close friends left. I'm 24 years old, and I live with my parents. I'm tired of playing peacemaker with them and calming my stepfather down. I have a useless degree, and I'm in the middle of getting what might be another worthless piece of paper. All I wanted out of life was someone to share it with. I wanted to start a family. Regrettably, after my most recent relationships with Gabrielle and Julie, I learned it's impossible to trust in a relationship, whether it's just a few months or several years.

My mother and father were married for more than ten years before they got divorced. I wouldn't be able to handle being constantly unsure if a relationship is going to end even after a decade or two of marriage. What kind of life is that? I try to treat women well, but if they want to break up without talking things out or just suddenly stop loving me, what can I do? Television, books, and movies all hype true love and happily ever after, but that doesn't exist. Relationships take work and communication, but I feel like I'm the only one who knows that and wants to put in the effort. I started out a hopeless romantic, but just ended up without hope.

C

"Screw me over once, shame on you. Screw me over twice, more shame on you."

Book of Ley

Tuesday February 21, 2006

Final Email to Gabrielle

Gabrielle,

By the time you read this, I will have killed myself. This will really be my last email. I gave Ed a sealed envelope yesterday with instructions and my last wishes. There are several things I am leaving to you, and part of the instructions for him was to call you later today.

I am sending you this because I wanted to give you a more detailed goodbye and a fuller explanation. I only wish you had let me talk to you in person instead of breaking up through instant messenger. I think that in itself might have been enough, but maybe not. There was a lot more bad stuff going on in my life, especially recently, that I wanted to tell you, but I never got the chance. I tried to put a smiling face on everything, but it was eating me up inside and getting to the point where there wasn't much left I could handle. It started getting worse not that long before you started feeling uncomfortable. I know you're very perceptive; perhaps subconsciously you noticed. I didn't feel like myself inside or outside any more, unlike earlier in our relationship. I didn't understand why you loved me one week and then stopped loving me a week later, but perhaps this was why. I should have stayed on Friday night and talked. It was foolish of me to just leave, but I was just upset and overwhelmed with everything. I just needed to clear my head.

I want you to know that this is not your fault. I'm an adult and responsible for my own decisions. The breakup was just the straw that broke the camel's back. I never fully got over Julie, and this just compounded that, on top of everything else. I never stopped loving her, and until the end of my life, I loved you. I was briefly happy during my time with you. I truly wish you all the best in life.

C

"Love is the root of all good."

Book of Ley

Journal: Monday January 16, 2006
I Love You

I remember the night Gabrielle first told me she loved me, just a few days after my 24th birthday. I was so surprised; I took almost an hour to respond, but I meant every word:

"I care so very much about you. When you're hurt, I hurt, and I want to wrap my arms around you and protect you from all the bad things in life or even just to give you the support you need to deal with them yourself. During the summer, I spent a lot of time thinking about what love is. I loved Julie and a small part of me will always love her, even though we were not right for each other. She left me with a huge hole in my heart that you have covered over. You treat me the way I deserve to be treated. There's a small part of me that wants to hold back because of fear you might change like Julie did, but you treat me better than she ever did. If love means you want to spend every moment of the day with someone, if it means she is the first thing you think about in the morning and the last thing you want to think about at night, if it means looking into her eyes and seeing how wonderful she'd be as the mother of your children, if it means her smile lights the room and your world, and if it means the mere thought of her makes you smile, then, yes, I love you."

Journal: Wednesday January 4, 2006
The Great Life

Life is still going extremely well. Gabrielle is now my girlfriend (as of 12/12), and I'm falling in love with her. On Friday, she'll meet my parents, and next Saturday, she'll meet my step-grandparents and my step-great aunt.

Next Friday is my birthday. 24 years old. Two dozen. Hard to believe. I'm going to Medieval Times with Ed, Beth, and Gabrielle to celebrate. Should be fun.

I've forgiven Tony, and from his hazy, confusing, rambling email, I think he might eventually want to be friends again. As long as everyone can be cordial at Ed and Beth's wedding, though, that's all I care about. I still believe he pled guilty because he was mostly guilty, and I know he's still a lying hypocrite. In spite of that, I wish him and Megan well, and I'm very happy for them now that they have a baby on the way.

"Learn from the past, and plan for the future, but don't ignore the present."

Book of Ley

Old Endings & New Beginnings

As the year comes to a close, I can't help but reflect on everything that has happened this past year, more specifically the last 6.5 months. Nothing has gone according to plan. In June, I was engaged and going to be married next October, had just moved into a nicer, more spacious apartment closer to my family and best friend, thought I was part of a close knit three couple group of friends, and was planning on going back to grad school in September to get a masters degree to be a high school English teacher.

During the summer (when I was teaching archery to campers in Michigan), my fiancée and I broke up. When I came back to NJ, I had to move back in my parents (after 5 years of living away) and found out that almost all of my friends betrayed me over the summer. I sunk into a black hole of depression, anger, and aggression, especially toward the one "friend" who, in my eyes, dealt me a very low blow by instigating and interfering where he didn't have a right to be.

Until last month, the only part of my life where I was making progress was physically. My anger and aggression led me to start working out almost religiously. I'm now in the best shape of my life, benching more than my body weight and curling with a 50 lb dumbbell.

Career wise, I'm going back to my true and original calling: counseling psychology. I'm applying to two PsyD programs and three MA/MS programs for Fall 2006. I want to counsel troubled youth.

Friend wise, I finally feel comfortable again with my best friend's fiancée, who was my friend when I introduced them three years ago, and I am now very much looking forward to being the best man at their wedding. We were once good friends, and I truly hope we will be again. Things went really well when they met my new girlfriend. I'm feeling optimistic that the four of us will have fun together many times in the future.

Gabrielle, my new girlfriend. She was the catalyst I needed to jerk me out of my depression. We met on a Jewish dating site. I had gone on too many crappy dates in the past few months and was about to just concentrate on trying to work myself out of my hole. I had already stopped paying for one site, and my date with Gabrielle was going to be one of my last from the Jewish site. I had a feeling from her profile and our conversations that she was going to be different and took her out to dinner on our first date instead of just meeting for drinks. There was a spark.

It was that spark that helped light my way out of my hole. I changed a lot in the last three years (in some ways better; in others, worse). I've been working on recovering the things about myself that were better then and reintegrating them into who I am now to be the best person I can be. I've returned to my calm, relaxed personality baseline that I lost towards the end of the summer. I'm even thinking about reaching out to the former friend who I felt hurt me most.

It may not always seem like it, but things happen for a reason. My life made a nice downward spiral for a little bit, but I can honestly say that things are now better than they were when I thought life was great 6.5 months ago. I'm with a woman who is more compatible with my values and personality, I feel like I can actually trust all of my friends, I'm heading down the career path I originally dreamed I would, and I even have a better relationship with my parents!

I hope this past month is only the start of a trend of good happenings that will continue in 2006! Happy Chanukah and Happy New Year!

Journal: Tuesday December 20, 2005

The Good Life

Life is going <u>extremely</u> well.

Journal: Tuesday December 13, 2005
Flowers at Work

Today I sent Gabrielle some flowers at work. A romantic little red rose bush in a pink foil-wrapped pot.

The attached card: *May these roses bask in your radiance and blossom in the presence of your beauty, like my heart when I'm with you.*

"Not all demons are ugly on the outside but all angels are beautiful on the inside."

Book of Ley

Gabrielle

Gazing into her hazelly-green eyes

Admiring her flowing tresses

Breathless from her beauty

Ready to live again

Infatuated by her sensuous curves

Enraptured by her soul

Lusting for her gentle caress

Longing for her silky soft lips

Enchantress of my heart

"Hope for the best, but prepare for the worst."

Book of Ley

Journal: Thursday December 8, 2005

A Decent Date

I should write in here more often; it's very therapeutic. I don't know what happened with the girl I went to high school with; I haven't heard from her in several weeks. I thought I made a new friend, but I guess I was wrong.

On the dating front, I've gone on quite a few dates in the last month or so, but only one went really well. Last Friday, I went out with Gabrielle. She's truly nice, sweet, and genuine. The date went perfectly. I brought her a single red rose, and we had dinner at the Olive Garden. Then we saw *Pride and Prejudice*. We held hands and made out during the movie. It was a great night.

Tomorrow I'm going to her place. We've talked a lot online, especially this past week when I was home with my cold, and I think we're forming a strong connection and would be a good match. If things go well tomorrow, I'll ask Gabrielle to be my girlfriend (either at the end of the date or the beginning of the next one).

The amazing positiveness of last Friday was the catalyst I need to end my depression. I'm no longer so angry at Tony that I want to beat the crap out of him, and I no longer care about eventually getting back together with Julie. Hopefully things will work out with Gabrielle, but if not, it won't matter too much. Getting my graduate degree in counseling psychology comes first.

Physically, I'm in the best shape of my life. In a few weeks I'll be benching my body weight. I'm curling with a 47.5 lb dumbbell; next week it'll be 50 lbs. I look good, and I feel good.

"Life is like a peanut; it's not a pea, and it's not a nut."

Book of Ley

Reality is a Harsh, Cold Mistress

I'm not stupid. Just wildly optimistic at times because it's better to lose oneself in hope than realize reality is a harsh, cold mistress. Other times, like now, the despair just slaps me in the face and overwhelms me. I've lost my chance at happiness; truthfully, I helped kill it through neglect. Now there's no one I can truly talk to, just the voices in my head, pounding away. The mind is deeply divided, between a hopeful optimist who sees the future achievement of all goals and dreams, and the logical rationalist who pulls back the curtain, revealing the true bleakness and abject misery and desolation that awaits.

The idealist and the cynic constantly battle it out, tempting me with happiness and truth and forcing me to choose. Unfortunately the happiness is blind, and the truth is cold. The cynic is winning and makes me long for what I lost and know I can never have again, and what I want but will not get, no matter how zealously I may try. There will always be a new rock to climb, a new raging river to cross. Life is a series of never-ending obstacles, and the only way to end the unremitting consecution of blockages placed along one's path is to stop the journey. Afraid to end the journey, but stuck under a crushing obstruction. Like Hamlet's lament, not choosing is itself a choice. The black hand of despair points towards a decision that would end all others. Sometimes seemingly a Hobson's choice, the option to end the forlornness tantalizes with its ease. Others would be affected, only a handful would truly care. A small voice yells out not to quit the journey before it ends but is barely detectable under the oppressive gloominess. Trying to clutch onto that voice like a drowning man but the heavy hopelessness pulls and drags. Over my head, and it's hard to breathe. Hard to see and hard not to sink. Only one end in sight and the other too far.

The mask of the optimist makes me lie to the world. Inside I'm scared, despondent, and lost. Barely hanging on to the last few threads that are starting to fray.

I thought I was good; I thought I was kind. But the actions of others are making me doubt. Do they merely not see me, or do they know me too well? Despite claims to the former, I quite fear the latter. I thought things were over that had only begun. No truly new beginnings. Just one major end. Sharp and piercing or calm and peaceful? Memorable and frightening or slow and serene?

Falling and falling with no one to catch. Down to the last and time's running out. A cry for attention or pleading for help? The laughter is gone; tears flow from the eyes. Afraid no one cares, but scared it's the truth. Curled in a ball, doubting the point of it all. Can no longer fake it; unable to hide. A broken little man; smashed pieces inside.

Things are not better; things are just worse. Time marches on like a damning foul curse. Looking for guidance, but scared of the truth. Nothing quite left, just a foul, gaping wound. Nothing good now and doubts about soon. Nothing left but pain and despair.

All I've done here is write how I feel.

"Life is like a mug of beer; sometimes it's overflowing, sometimes it's almost empty, and once in a while it has a huge fly doing the backstroke."

Book of Ley

Journal: Wednesday November 16, 2005
New Job

Last week I started my new job as a test evaluator. It's mind-numbing work. I stare at a computer screen all day grading essays on a scale of 1 to 6. At least the pay is good, and I get to work with Ed. I took off today to tutor in the morning and go to the eye doctor in the afternoon.

I'm going to have dinner with my old friend from high school tonight after my appointment. I called her twice after we went out last time and never heard from her until Ed and I ran into her again last week. This time I was smart enough to get her email address and screen name. I really like her, and I hope things go well tonight. It's always good to gain a new friend. ☺

Of course, I'm still in love with Julie and plan to try to win her back in the months before Ed and Beth's wedding or at their wedding. I know my chances are slim, but I have to try. I love her.

"The waters of eternity are constantly washing up at the sands of time."

Book of Ley

Journal: Thursday October 13, 2005

Yom Kippur

Today is Yom Kippur, day of fasting and repentance. I feel closer to G-d at the moment. Today I will ask for forgiveness from Beth for my comment about not being sure of her love for Ed.

Even though I'm sad about Julie (and still love her), I'm excited that I'm forming new connections with women and getting out there. On Saturday, I have a date in Princeton. I haven't had a first date in four years (since Tina). Julie and I just had our meeting each other turn into a date at some point that evening. I miss her. I'm also going to get together with a girl I went to high school with. Ed and I ran into her a few weeks ago. I'm hoping to make a new friend 'cause my current ones seem to be few and far between.

"It's easy to vilify a person when you can't see the pain and anguish in his eyes."

Book of Ley

Wrongness

I feel an immense sense of wrongness. Things are not right. I have a very bad feeling/premonition that Ed and Beth are going to break up. I try to picture their wedding next year, and I can't. It's as if everything is falling apart.

I'm way too self-aware. It's so easy to drown myself in books, but is that really a good answer? Even though it's the most socially acceptable means of escape, it's still an escape from reality.

"Better to be Socrates dissatisfied than a fool satisfied." At least the fool can be happy in his ignorance.

"I may be a man, and you may be a woman. I may have light skin, and you may have dark skin. I may be a Jew, and you may be a Catholic. But, first and foremost, we are all human beings."

Book of Ley

I'm Telling You This As Your Friend

Beth,

You've told me that friends should tell each other what they need to hear, no matter how hard it is to do, and that we should always keep things out in the open and not let things bubble over. That's why I'm writing this email.

I just read your away message about cutting off all relationships and spoke to Ed about what happened tonight. You know I was telling the whole truth about Tony, and you know the things he's done. It was your choice to give him a second (third?) chance. You're an adult and can make your own choices. With everything you know about Tony and what's happened in both the past and present, I am truly shocked that would end things with both him and Ed instead of standing with your fiancée. It blows my mind.

In my opinion, when someone loves somebody, s/he should treat that relationship as the most important one. You could respond to this with comments about my relationship with Julie, but I think that subject was exhausted by you and Tony over the summer. Of course, even now there's still a little you don't know about what happened with our relationship, but I will tell you that one of the reasons Julie and I were having problems is because I was treated like I was quite far down on her list of important relationships. But that's something for another day. I personally don't understand how you could consider your relationships with Ed and Tony to be equally important, especially with all of Tony's "behaviors."

I know you're sick, and I really hope you feel better, but you said not to let things fester. Right now, I'm really disgusted with myself at my choice of friends. Tony showed me his true colors this summer, and now I know you're not the person I thought you were. You might not like me very much after this email, but at least I've been upfront (and will continue to be). I may be arrogant and lazy, but at least my friends can count on me to be upfront with them.

Ed is my best friend, and I love him like a brother. I want him to be happy, and I want him to be with the woman who will make him happy. He loves you, and you say you love him. I don't want to see him hurt. Please don't hurt him.

C

"You are unique, just like everyone else. Does this mean you're special or just expendable?"

Book of Ley

Journal: Sunday September 25, 2005

Nothing

I feel pretty depressed and useless. I'm going crazy. I have nothing I really look forward to.

"Not knowing yourself is like living in a two-story house and never going beyond the first floor."

Book of Ley

Journal: Friday September 23, 2005
What Do I Want?

What do I want in life?

What I Want

1) Woman
2) Kids
3) Friends
4) Job I Like With Decent $
5) House

I need #4 to get #1, which will lead to #2 and #5 and cement #3.

Journal: Friday September 23, 2005
Some Friends?

I might actually get to keep Beth as a friend. That would be nice. I only wish she'd take off her rose-colored glasses and open her eyes to what is really going on with Tony.

I have a second interview (along with Ed) on Tuesday for a financial advisor position. I could make some very good money with this job.

If I take this job, maybe I could win Julie back in a year. Do I want Julie back? I don't know. I've been having dreams about her.

"You are free to disagree with anything I say, provided you respect my right to say it."

Book of Ley

Beth,

I've laid all my cards on the table. At this point, most anything I could say would just be a reiteration of the issues I've mentioned previously. I would, however, like to address your point that we should accept people for who they are, flaws and all. I agree with that, but only to a certain point. Tony lied to me repeatedly and on numerous occasions, sometimes about very stupid things. This is not just a matter of different interpretations; I have the actual words he used. I cannot be friends with someone when I know he will lie right to my face and I can't believe half the words that are coming out of his mouth. I told Tony this, and he lied to me not even 24 hours later (about the dinner). There's a huge difference between accepting someone's flaws and turning a blind eye when he's doing things you know are morally reprehensible (the lying and the pattern of inappropriate behavior, of which I doubt you're even fully aware).

While saying that I'm the only one who has "rocked the boat" is technically true, it significantly downplays the fact that what I was (and am) doing was (and is) just being honest and upfront, something both you and Tony claim is important and claim you do, yet fail to follow up on (you simply keeping things inside; Tony keeping things inside and lying). It makes me quite sad that I'm basically getting crapped on for being the only one actually doing what all of you say we should be doing. I was also sad over the fact that, while I was gone over the summer, quite a few bad things were said about me that I was unable to defend myself against. It's also been upsetting me that Julie has said a few untrue things, especially when Ed saw with his own eyes the truth.

You also said, "… because G-d knows that the worst has been drawn out in all of us." While I have done wrong things in the past (sometimes very wrong things), I can actually come out of this situation with a clear conscience. I have been truthful and upfront, and while some of the stuff I've said has been hurtful, that is ONLY because it was true. I have tried to keep everything on a dignified and civil level without resorting to name calling or insults, especially untrue ones where the other person isn't even there to respond.

As far as getting to know me better and knowing the kind of person I am goes, Ed is the only one you should really be listening to. He knows me better than anyone, even about the bad stuff, and knows the full story. Or even just talk to me one-on-one. You know everyone else will be biased in the negative direction, and, by the way, I have proof that Tony has lied about me, in terms of negative things (involving Ed, so Ed is quite aware of this as well). Even to my face (figuratively, also includes phone and IM conversations), Tony has said some pretty nasty things to me about me. I am by no means saying should choose between Tony and myself; rather, I am presenting the facts so you come to your own conclusions and resolve them to your satisfaction with him, if necessary. I would even happily have you come here to see these things for yourself so you can know 100% that I'm telling the truth. Basically, all I ask as your friend is that you take a good, hard look at the facts, without simply taking sides because you've known Tony longer, or because you don't like me, or because you're very close to Megan and Julie and I'm easier to end things with.

Except for what has been going on in terms of this situation and about you not letting me know how you truly felt about me, I think you're a wonderful person, and I'm glad Ed will be spending the rest of his life with you. I want to remain your friend and be closer with you in the future, especially when I find someone new to be with so we can go out as two couples again.

Your friend,

C

Beth,

Ed told me you were concerned about this sentence from the email I wrote Tony: "I was only trying to patch things up and give our friendship another shot so Ed and Beth could have a somewhat civil wedding party on their special day because they both mean a great deal to me." To clarify, I was basically saying that it would be best for you and Ed if there weren't tensions between the members of the wedding party. I would never, ever, cause a scene at your wedding. You and Ed mean way too much to me. Ed told me about the ultimatum from Tony and Megan where he will be forced to make a choice. I love Ed like a brother. He means so much to me that I only want him to be happy, and I told him he should choose them so you can be happy. I am aware of the way you feel about me, but until you tell me otherwise, I will consider you one of my closest friends. I care about you a great deal. Because of this, and because I know Ed only wants you to be happy, I told him I completely understand if you no longer want me as best man or in the wedding party (although it would sadden me greatly).

The only other thing I want to say is that what I said in the email to Tony was completely true and provable (to anyone's satisfaction), and I stand by it completely. I am not trying to create "drama" (as Tony has been calling it); rather, I have been the ONLY one of our little group who has been completely honest and upfront about everything with all of you in spite of all of you making claims about how important it is to be honest with one's friends. There's more I could say, but I don't want to create any more "drama." Please don't feel like you need to choose between Tony & Megan and myself.

Your loving friend,

C

Journal: Sunday September 18, 2005
No More Friends

No more Tony, Megan, or Beth. I'm afraid I'm going to lose Ed, too. They're going to make him choose/give him an ultimatum. I basically gave Ed permission to choose them over me because of Beth (since Megan is now her best friend).

I'm upset with lots of people, but oddly, I don't hate anyone. I don't know why. I'm even a little upset with myself. I feel like I should go far, far away to make life easier for everyone else.

"Everyone has the right to his/her own opinion, no matter how wrong, uninformed, or stupid it may be."

Book of Ley

Email: Sunday September 18, 2005

Our Friendship

Dear Anthony,

When we talked the other night, you said you were joking about a probationary period for our friendship. I wasn't. Our friendship is over. Less than 24 hours after our long talk, you lied again, and I have unalterable proof (seen by both Ed & Beth). It was stupid to lie about dinner; you didn't even have to invite me in the first place, although I hope Megan had a very happy birthday. I was only trying to patch things up and give our friendship another shot, so Ed and Beth could have a somewhat civil wedding party on their special day because they both mean a great deal to me.

You say that everything was good before I came home from camp and brought "drama" into everyone's lives. The truth is that I'm the only one willing to be open and honest about things. No one else wants to rock the boat. Ed is the one who brought up and questioned your conviction a few months ago. At first, I didn't even agree with him. Then I started thinking about things and realized there's a clear pattern of 4 incidents (at least that I'm aware of), and from observation, your behavior towards women can be quite inappropriate at times. Also, I don't know what you said to Ed this weekend, but he remains unconvinced of your innocence, and it sounds to me like he has even more doubts than before. I don't know how you managed that.

You've said that your friends shouldn't keep anything inside and should always be upfront with you because you're always upfront with them. That's not true; you've kept things hidden for way longer than anyone else would. You didn't say anything to me about how what happened in North Carolina made you not want to go out of your way to invite Julie and me to anything until ALMOST A YEAR LATER. You also didn't tell Julie that one of her comments made Megan uncomfortable until TWO YEARS LATER (which, by the way, really pissed Julie off, especially because of your hypocrisy about being "upfront").

You keep saying you're upfront and honest with everyone, but that's a lie right there. Not only do I have proof of your most recent lie about dinner, but I also have proof of several of your other lies; proof that was, and is, impossible to edit. Ed has seen everything and knows I could not have altered it in any way. Also, to save you the trouble of telling Ed and Beth about this email (and possibly altering it), I have taken the liberty of sending them copies as well. I hope Megan has a very happy and fulfilling life, and since that includes you, I wish you the same.

Your former friend,

C

"The roads to both Heaven and Hell are paved with good intentions, but Heaven's road is coated with the fulfillment of those intentions."

Book of Ley

Journal: Tuesday September 6, 2005

My Car Reflects My Life

Once again, I'm waiting for my car to be fixed. I just had a very late lunch at a pizza place down the street from the car repair shop. Tim from the repair shop just called me to say the wrong part was sent over, so the car won't be ready until tomorrow morning.

Apparently, the fuel injectors need to be replaced, and it's gonna cost me about $500. At least I have enough in my checking account to cover it.

To recap my wonderful situation, I have no woman, no job, a car that keeps breaking down, a rapidly dwindling amount of money, and I live with my parents. At least I'm relatively healthy, and I have my family and a couple friends.

I found out from Ed that there's no chance for me to get back together with Julie, even if she does love me. I don't think I love her. I get feelings for her when I look at pictures and cards, but that's it. I just care about her and wish her well.

Mainly, I'm very lonely. I miss Rebecca. Odd/funny that I would miss her more than Julie. I wonder how things would have been different if I gave Julie the neck and back massages I gave Rebecca?

I get conflicting signals about how Rebecca feels about me, so I don't know if there's any future there.

I'm going crazy because I don't know what to do with myself. Other than a sense of responsibility, I don't really care about having a job. Mainly I want someone to be with, to love. I want a family: wife, kids, house, dog.

I feel like Ed a little in that I'd just like to have enough money so I wouldn't have to work. If I did, I'd probably write. I just need to train myself to sit down and actually crank out a certain number of pages in a set amount of time.

I feel like I have no control over my life. Things are happening that I did not expect or want. Major things. I didn't leave in June expecting to be in this situation when I got back.

I'm surprised the Army hasn't called me yet. That could be promising, and it's much better than killing myself. Three years of active duty isn't that much.

I'm thinking about calling my unit head from camp in a few weeks to ask him about jobs out in Michigan. I hope he's doing well.

Interviews

I'm waiting for my car to get an oil change, a tune-up, and some things fixed. Should be done soon.

I drove down to Maryland on Thursday for a job interview with a learning center for an assistant director position. I found out last night that I didn't make it to the next round of interviews. I have one more interview scheduled a school near Boston on Tuesday September 13th. The position is program aide and pays $10.75, but I can also get room and board if I stay in three nights a week, plus there's tuition assistance available.

I'm also thinking about joining the military. Now is the perfect time. I have no obligations and nothing to tie me down. I can leave all my stuff at my parents' house. I could be an officer. It's definitely an option to consider.

"The more I wonder how, the more I ask why."

Book of Ley

Journal: Monday August 29, 2005

What I Want in Life

I'm finally adjusting to living without Julie, but I'm very lonely. I still have feelings for Rebecca, which doesn't help, as I doubt she feels similarly towards me.

I've been thinking about what I want in life. The very top of the list is love and companionship. Job, money, etc. are all meaningless without it. Unfortunately, if I want someone to love who will love me back, I need a job, some money, independence from my parents, and an eventual career.

I think I need to move away. I'm starting to get a taste of what life will be like here with Ed teaching and Beth working. Ed is the only one I feel really close to. He's the only one I can share everything with. I can say exactly how I feel or what I think and not be though of negatively for it.

Part of me just wants to sit here and die. Another part just wants to run away—destination unknown. Another part wants to go see Rebecca.

I'm going crazy and my handwriting is getting very funky and off-the-wall. I look in the mirror, and I see a stranger staring back at me. I can't believe I'm an adult. This is not what I wanted to be at age 23.

Journal: Sunday August 21, 2005

Trouble Sleeping

      I've been very depressed during the night, and I've had trouble sleeping. Hopefully that will end now that I have a goal. I'm going to apply for a ton of jobs and hope I can get one ASAP so I can talk to Julie on more equal footing. In the morning, I'm going to apply for the 25 jobs I have saved online.

      At 10:30 A.M., Ed is going to pick me up, and I'm going to go to the shore with him and Beth. I could use some time to relax with all the stress I've been under.

Journal: Monday August 8, 2005
The Letter

Last night I wrote a letter to Julie's parents and sister, thanking them for treating me like a part of their family and telling them I'd miss them a lot.

Tony, Megan, and Beth are all firmly in Julie's camp. Ed is the only one who sides with me. He'll be the only one I really miss when I move if/when I move away.

I'm not sure what to do about Rebecca. Part of me wants to go for it, and part of me thinks it's too soon, and I'm not really interested in a long-distance relationship.

"Life is like a coin; just when you think it's going to land either tails up or heads up, it lands right on its edge and really messes you up."

Book of Ley

No Woman

I might wind up with no female companionship when I get home. That would be quite ironic. From trying to decide between two women to having none.

"When life throws you a lemon, throw it back and pick an apple."

Book of Ley

Journal: Thursday August 4, 2005
New Start

I've come to accept that I have very little to come back to. Just my friends and family. I shouldn't say "just," but a lot of other stuff is no longer there.

I'm going to have to make a fresh start. It's actually starting to feel a little exciting. I'm applying for jobs. Basically, wherever I get a job is where I'll go. Find a job. Find an apartment. Start over.

I'm really starting to have strong feelings for Rebecca. My desire for her is almost overwhelming. I want to sweep her off her feet. Grab her firmly but gently. Bend her back slightly. Press my lips up against hers.

Break Up

Julie broke up with me last night. Actually, it was pretty mutual; she just brought it up first. Even though I saw it coming and know it was for the best, I'm still upset.

Journal: Wednesday July 27, 2005

Questions To Ponder

There are several questions I need to ask myself and ponder:

- Do I still love Julie?
- If so, can I foresee loving Rebecca more?
- Does the risk outweigh the reward or vice versa?
- Can I see a happy future with Julie?
- Can I see a future with Rebecca?
- Am I willing to put in the work necessary to fix things with Julie?
- Do I still have a chance at fixing things with Julie, or is it past redemption?
- Does Julie love me?
- Does Rebecca have feelings for me?
- If I try things with Rebecca, am I willing to risk everything (if I still have it left to lose)?
- Am I willing to move to another state?
- Am I willing to move back in with my parents (might not have a choice)?
- If I try something with Rebecca and it fails, would I lose her as a friend?

Journal: Wednesday July 27, 2005

No Home

I feel horrible inside. Torn between several vastly different futures where the main decision involves others. I'm falling in love with Rebecca, but I think I still love Julie.

Even though we agreed not talk until I get home, Julie left me a voicemail message tonight that said she doesn't want me to come back to the apartment and that she prefers that I go to my parents' house.

Although it might not be the happiest path, at least I can see a fairly close future with Julie and a close move into the next stage of life.

Rebecca is still growing as a person and has another three years of school left. She could easily be a different person in a few years.

"If it looks like duck, walks like a duck, and quacks like a duck, there's a small chance it might just be a cow with a duck complex."

Book of Ley

Journal: Monday July 25, 2005

Devolving Into Arguments

It's been a roller coaster ride of a week. On Thursday night I thought Julie and I broke up. Over the phone I asked her how she could love me and not miss me, and that if she doesn't love me, why are we even getting married? She hung up and left a message an hour and a half later saying she didn't feel angry, sad, or upset. She just felt relieved at what I said.

I was a mess the rest of that night and Friday morning. I made it through the day and started to feel relieved myself and beginning to look forward to a new future.

I found out on Saturday morning that Julie didn't mean for what she said to be taken that way. I wish she would think about how other people would react to the words that come out of her mouth.

When we talked on the phone, it just devolved into an argument. We decided to have a break for the next three and a half weeks (until the end of camp).

She didn't even want me to come home early so we could talk things out. We're not going to even talk until I get home.

In my eyes, the relationship is mostly over.

"There's a thin line between interesting and seriously fucked up."

Book of Ley

Journal: Wednesday July 20, 2005
Go Home?

I almost went home yesterday. The camp director said he understood that I missed Julie, said my pay would be prorated, and told me I'd be welcome back next year. He also said how wonderful a counselor I was and mentioned how I was the only counselor who had to climb over kids (guess he didn't notice Rebecca) to leave the auditorium to prepare the staff song. The real reason I want to go home now is because I know something will happen with Rebecca within the next month.

Something my mom said actually convinced me to stay. I expected her to be thrilled to have me come home early. Instead, she said that even though she misses me and would be happy to have me come home, I made a commitment and should stick to it. That's what I'm going to do.

When Julie finally called me back today, she seemed very upset that I considered coming home early. She also implied that she didn't miss me all that much and said that she missed her parents more because she lived with them for 18 years and only lived with me for 2.

I'm starting to feel like she doesn't love me very much and doesn't really care whether I eventually come home or not.

At least Rebecca lets me touch her in public and is very good-natured. This isn't a choice I want to make. I feel like running away, but I'm an adult, which sometimes sucks.

Journal: Saturday July 16, 2005

Animal Magnetism

I thought my feelings for Rebecca were lessening, but they're slowly increasing. I've chosen Julie, and I love Julie, so I really don't want to pursue anything with Rebecca. I feel this really strong magnetic attraction to her. I just want to put my arms around her and feel the soft press of her lips against mine.

Journal: Wednesday July 13, 2005
Sweet Release

My feelings for Rebecca have abated somewhat. A month without release was just too much. At least now I'm not a horny bastard. I really miss Julie, and I can't wait to get home. I'm afraid something still might happen with Rebecca, but at least the urge isn't overwhelming now.

Overwhelmed

The attraction is growing stronger. My mind is reeling, and I feel totally overwhelmed.

Journal: Tuesday July 5, 2005
Two of Everything

When I was a little kid, I always wanted two of everything. Two balloons. Two toys. Two stuffed animals. Now I find myself wanting two women. So close physically and in personality, but the small differences are the important ones that make me question whether or not I made the right decision before meeting Rebecca. I love Julie, but I find myself falling for Rebecca. If only Rebecca didn't have most of the things I love about Julie, I wouldn't have this problem. I keep deciding to stick with Julie, but 9 weeks is a long time. How strong is my self-control? It's only been 3 weeks, but the more time I spend with Rebecca, the deeper our connection gets. Even if I can't/won't start a relationship with Rebecca, I want to have her as a friend.

Julie. Rebecca. Julie. Rebecca. Julie. Rebecca. Julie.

It's too hard being an adult. A responsible adult anyway. Although I don't condone it, I now know why people cheat (sexually and emotionally) and can definitely sympathize. Maybe I just need more to do?

At least I know I'm not delusional; everyone at camp thinks we'd make a great match. My kids even thought I was married to Rebecca before I set them straight.

"Sometimes you have to make the wrong choices just to get an opportunity to make the right one."

Book of Ley

Two Paths

When is love enough?

How much love is enough?

How can love even be measured?

It's all relative and subjective.

Two paths.

Both paved with happiness and regrets.

Both right.

Both wrong.

Neither quite right.

Stumble along.

Journal: Thursday April 11, 2004

Toys

Yesterday I stopped in a few stores to do a little shopping. I went into a toy store to buy a few games because they've been having some great sales (going out of business soon). I saw two particular items with a retail price of $9.99 each. That made me want to cry because I used to sell them for $20 to $30 and say they had a retail price of $40 each. Just because I was also lied to about the price didn't make me feel any better.

Journal: Monday March 29, 2004
3-Month Update

It's been three months since I've written in here; I really need to use this journal more often. Lots of stuff happened.

Had a job for two months. I worked at a marketing company doing event marketing and providing free fingerprinting for kids. I sold toys, safety items, and other products. I became a team leader and went on a business trip to Virginia. Unfortunately, some things at the company made me somewhat suspicious. I brought up my suspicions and told them, if my concerns weren't addressed, I was thinking of quitting. Basically, I was told I just did. Later on, I found out lots of horrible things about the company. I thought I was doing something good and worthwhile; turns out I was doing just the opposite.

In January, I celebrated my 22nd birthday with friends and family at a nice place in NJ. Food, dancing, lots of fun. For Valentine's Day, Julie and I stayed in and watched movies from the video store. Julie made us a feast.

I was not accepted to the two graduate school programs I applied to. I had to contact them; I still haven't received an official rejection letter from either school. I was only told that the people they were interested in already came for interviews. Guess I have to wait until next year when I can apply to programs farther out.

Journal: Wednesday December 31, 2003
6-Month Update

It's been over 6 months since I've written in here. Much has happened. Where to start? Jon and Kana were married on Sun. Oct. 12th. It was a beautiful affair, and I gave a wonderful speech. Julie and I danced a lot. I hope our wedding goes as well as Jon and Kana's. The month after, on Sat. Nov. 29th, Jon and George (mainly George), threw Barb and Stan a surprise 50th anniversary party. Julie and I made collages of them and the family. It's weird; I've known George, Jon, Barb, and Stan since I was 4 years old. George does all the things a father is supposed to do, I consider Jon my uncle, and I think of Barb and Stan as real grandparents, but I still feel like an outsider and an imposter. Maybe I'll write more about that later.

Also that day (Sat. Nov. 29th), Ed proposed to Beth on the 1-year anniversary of their first date. Best friends engaged to best friends. Life is crazy like that. Ed and Beth are planning to get married spring 2006 (yep, a few months before Julie and I).

Julie and I also celebrated the 1-year anniversary of when we met, as well as the 1-year anniversary of when I proposed (Sept. 27th and Oct.6th, respectively). Things were going well. We had a great vacation over X-mas in Atlantic City. We stayed right on the boardwalk. I got a good deal on a junior suite at the Royal Suites at the Atlantic Palace, where every suite has a Jacuzzi in the bathroom. We got lucky at the casinos, then other places, like in the Jacuzzi, on the window seat, on the floor, and on the bed. The sex during the trip and since (so far) has been amazing.

Unfortunately, Julie and I are in the middle of a huge fight, mainly because I feel she's not being very supportive during this very stressful time in my life. I'm looking for a job I can do for 9 months or maybe a year and 9 months (even not knowing how long is stressful). Yesterday I was offered a job as a youth counselor (in both senses of the word). If circumstances were a little different, it would be the perfect job. I'm going to have to tell them I can't take the job. That's one of the hardest decisions I've ever had to make in my life. With the unusual schedule and the long commute, I'd barely see Julie. I'm depressed about my decision, but I know it's the right one. If I took this job, work would be my life. I will never be like my stepfather; work will never be the most important thing in my life. Julie, family, and friends are the most important things in my life, and they will always come before work.

Happier news: since I'm looking for a job, obviously I graduated. Summer '03 my GPA was a 4.0 (wow), and Fall '03 was a 3.8. I graduated with a 3.8, which means I graduated with the second level of honors (magna cum laude). My major GPA was a 3.9, and my minor GPA was a 4.0. Plus I graduated in three and a third years (technically class of '03) and with distinction from the honors college.

I had a graduation party on Sat. Dec. 20th in Cherry Hill. My mom, Julie, and Ed all gave nice speeches. Julie made me a cool sign-in board. It was a fun party, but it would have been better with the rest of my family. Bart had a heart attack the week before and was just leaving the hospital the day of my party. I'm so glad he caught it quickly and had Harriet drive him to the hospital, so the damage was minimal. It was such a surprise because he's so young (only in his early fifties) and works out regularly. When Julie and I visited him in the hospital, he seemed to still be in a state of shock (could have been the meds) and said it was a life-altering event. I hope that means he's going to propose to Harriet. I'm already looking forward to Ed and Beth's wedding and Tony and Megan's wedding. I'd love to have one more to look forward to attending.

"Life is messy. Real life resolutions are never tidy or complete."

Book of Ley

Journal: Tuesday May 27, 2003
Some Issues

Today was the eight-month anniversary of when Julie and I met. I gave her five deep pink roses. We spend the weekend at our new apartment, and then went back to my old on-campus apartment. We had a major fight, and she said/wrote some very mean things. There was a lot of yelling last night, and she's afraid to show her face to my roommates again, but we made up.

I don't know when I'll be in the mood again to have sex with her; the things she said about our sex life were pretty horrible and mean, even if she didn't mean them. It's easy to forgive, but hard to forget. Apparently, she's meanest to those she loves the most and bitchiest right before her period. I'll have to subtly help her work out these issues because I don't want to have to deal with this crap for the rest of my life. I love her, though, and that's the most important thing.

On Friday, Julie, Kelly, Ed, Beth, and I hung out at the new apartment, and I made them a nice home-cooked meal: tuna fish and pasta shells, egg salad, and peas. We played board games, went to the Cosi on 12th St., and then saw a movie.

Last Sunday, we moved the furniture from my parents' house (my parents, Kelly, Ed, and I). Julie and Beth were at their leadership retreat. In the moving truck, my stepfather said something that really hurt: he's stuck with me and he's been stuck with me for the last 17 years. Later in the week, he apologized and claimed he didn't mean it, but who knows?

Overall, I suppose the week wasn't all that good.

Journal: Thursday March 15, 2003

Moving In

Today Julie and I signed the lease and picked up the keys to our new apartment. I'm excited because it is a new step in my life. Living with the woman who will be my wife. Graduating college in a few months. It's all a little overwhelming, but definitely very exciting. Ed is going to help me start moving in a few hours.

Where does the time go???

Journal: Sunday March 5, 2003
Julie's Grandmother

I put Julie on the train to Massachusetts on Friday. I had to go up late Saturday evening because of Peer Counselor training. Today was the stone unveiling for Julie's grandmother. I came up here so I could comfort Julie and because it was the right thing to do. I think I would've liked her grandmother; from what was said about her, she sounded like a wonderful lady.

New Apartment

Over Spring Break, I slept over at Julie's apartment because her roommates were on a crew trip. We watched a lot of videos and had a lot of fun.

We also went apartment hunting that week and put down a deposit on a basement apartment in a brownstone in Center City. I move in on May 15th, in five weeks, and Julie will permanently move in sometime in August when her lease is up.

On the 30th, Julie's parents came down. They were in a car accident, but thankfully they weren't hurt. The car was totaled. We played board games. Afterward, we went to The Mexican Post for dinner. It's near Penn's Landing. It was good cheap food, and I would definitely recommend the place.

Last Monday, classes started. Julie and I are both taking 19 credits. I can't believe I'm graduating at the end of the fall term. Time flies. The first week of classes went well.

Sunday was the six-month anniversary of when I proposed. I took Julie to this modern/futuristic/sushi place for dinner and dessert. Their food was really excellent, but expensive. I really enjoyed the chocolate bento box we shared for dessert. Afterward we had a second dessert at Ben & Jerry's. I love Julie so much. Je t'aime et je t'adore, Julie.

Zoo & Sick

On Sunday, Julie and I went to the Philadelphia Zoo. It was her first time there. We saw lots of interesting animals and had tons of fun. I'll probably get the pictures developed this weekend. I bought Julie a cute frog magnet.

Last night I had my last final. I could've postponed it 'cause I was (and still am) sick, but I just wanted to get it over with already. I can barely hear out of my right ear. I went to the Student Health Center yesterday, and the doctor said what I have is definitely viral, but he prescribed meds to kill the stuff growing in my ears, throat, nose, and lungs. I think I got it in my ears because Julie was a little sick last week, and it turns me on when she licks my ears.

Journal: Thursday February 27, 2003

Dealing With Problems

On an unhappier note, I'm really getting tired of Julie having so many "downs." I probably feel this way because I think a person should just deal with his/her problems without always putting them out there to bring others down and letting those problems color everything. Telling people about problems is okay, and of course it's reasonable to be upset when extremely horrible happens, like when someone is sick or dies. But minor issues should just be accepted and dealt with. In my opinion, she needs to learn to handle her emotions instead of letting them handle her. I have my own problems, but I don't let them to get to me. I don't like my tremors and could definitely do without them. Those were the cards that were dealt, which are more than made up for by other cards, like the relationship I have with Julie (the Queen of Hearts). I don't know what I'd do without her. I love her so much.

Journal: Monday February 24, 2003
Dropping Eggs and Meeting Parents

On Friday, I took the egg container Beth and I designed to the Ninth Annual Kamikaze Egg Drop in the Main Building. Although we didn't place because our design was too heavy and slow, the egg survived both rounds. We were proud of that, and we now know a better design for next year.

On Saturday, Julie and I, and both sets of parents, went out to dinner at Oasis, a sushi buffet. I love their eel sushi. I tried the sushi with the baby octopus, but it tasted like it looked. Things went well (surprisingly?) between our parents, and my parents are going to treat next time.

The Gables

This weekend Julie and I went to a bed and breakfast in University City called The Gables. We stayed in a room called the Library. The breakfast (cooked by one of the owners) was delicious (quiche, scrambled eggs, muffins), and the house was beautifully Victorian. Last night, Julie and I went to the Mystery Café at the Bistro Romano for dinner and a murder mystery. It was okay, but I don't think we would have gone if we didn't have a coupon. All in all, it was a great weekend, very romantic, and made much more special by sharing it with the love of my life.

"Live every day as if it were your first, and you'll always be right."

Book of Ley

It is a new year, and nine days from now will be my most important milestone birthday: my 21st. Blackjack. It feels like a good time to start recording the events in my life, as well as my thoughts and feelings about those events and about the important people in my life. Before I write about them, let me fill in the details of who I am.

I am currently a junior at Drexel University in Philly, PA, and am anticipating a Dec. 2003 graduation. Psychology is my major and communication is my minor. I am in the honors program and am going to be inducted soon into Golden Key (an international honor society) and Psi Chi (a national psychology honors fraternity). I am an officer in the UCC (Undergraduate Class Council), and I recently completed training to be a WIT (Writing Intensive Tutor). I start Tues. My cum. GPA is currently 3.7, and my psych. GPA is currently around 3.8. After I graduate with my B.S. in psych., I plan to get a Ph.D. in education to become a career counselor and teach.

Physical data: 5'7", 140-145 lbs, brown hair, light brown eyes with random green flecks when I get excited (so I've been told), lean w/a slightly muscular build.

On Jan. 13th, 2003, I will turn 21. Even though that's a major event in my life, I care more about the wonderful people I know and love:

Julie – My beautiful and intelligent fiancée. She knows me better than anyone does, has, or ever will. I love her with all my heart. We met at Hillel on Sept. 27th, 2002, and I knew that very night that she was the woman I wanted to spend the rest of my life with. I proposed 9 days later on Oct. 6th, in Fairmount Park in the azalea garden behind the art museum. We are going to get married in early fall 2006 (most likely). As I write this, she is asleep next to me. We are spending the weekend at a bed and breakfast. She is my soul mate, my true love, and every day, I thank G-d that we are together. She makes life happier, brighter, infinitely better.

Edward/Ed – My best friend. We became friends senior year in high school, but knew each other through a mutual friend since 7th grade. Ed is originally from Germany, and he currently attends college at Princeton University in Princeton, NJ. He also wants to get a Ph.D. in education, like I do, but more because he wants to be a teacher or professor. Ed is dating Julie's closest friend, Beth (also my close friend). Not only is it weird that two best friends are in relationships with two best friends, but they make a strange (in a good way) couple: Ed is a 5'4" atheistic Jew, while Beth is a 5'10" religious Catholic. They look like Mutt and Jeff, but their personalities mesh well. Oh, I forgot to mention that Ed is double majoring in economics and sociology. He'll graduate Dec. 2003 with his B.A.

Elizabeth/Beth – One of my closest friends, Julie's closest friend, and Ed's girlfriend. Beth is a pre-junior at Drexel majoring in chemistry. She plans on going to medical school so she can become an anesthesiologist. She is a very religious Catholic and a very kind, caring person. It's great getting together the four of us for movies, games, and hanging out. I really enjoyed her Christmas party and New Year's party. It was the best New Year's I ever had. She is a friend I can trust and rely on. I really enjoy spending time with her, and I am glad she is my friend.

Julie

Jewel of my heart

Untamed lover

Love of my life

I need you

Enchantress

Thursday December 5, 2002
Love Changes Everything

Love
Changes Everything

Sunny day
To pitch-black night

Tiny ant
To gigantic hippo

Purest good
To darkest evil

Might oak
To little acorn

Arid desert
To roiling ocean

Love
Changes Everything

Roiling ocean
To arid desert

Darkest evil
To purest good

Gigantic hippo
To tiny ant

Pitch-black night
To sunny day.

Love
Changes Everything

Love Poem

The heat of your body warming up mine.

The bonfire ablaze in my heart.

Fingers through your silky brown hair.

One finger up and down your spine.

Backing away with a slight jump and a cute little noise.

Infectious laughter to melt my cares away.

Getting lost in your deep brown eyes.

Finding a matching soul.

Looking deep inside.

Drowning in the depths.

Floating on a cloud.

Flying with large leathery dragon wings.

My sweet silver dragon.

Your fuzzy brown dragon.

Take a step

To soar above the clouds.

Fall into the abyss

To grow wings.

Your Sleeping Form

For my sweet silver dragon, Julie
From your furry animal, C

As I gaze upon your sleeping form
Partially by the blankets hidden
My heart fills beyond the norm
And these words they come unbidden.

When our gaze locks
And I look into your eyes
I tingle with such pleasant shocks
And my whole body, it electrifies.

I love you so very, very much
That when I hold you close and tight
And feel your soft and gentle touch
I just know: everything is Right.

The Little Bird

Once upon a time
I heard a little rhyme.

Wasn't just a story
More . . . An allegory.

There was a tiny bird
He knew a single word.

A brown mourning dove
Just repeating . . . "Love."

Every female he annoyed
So him they did avoid.

Just a lonely little bird
With a simple little word.

He really was quite lonely
Searching for his one & only.

But his sad and solitary word
Went unrequited and unheard.

One day he had a novel thought
About the special thing he sought.

"Why, I'm just wasting my entire life away!"
But at that moment he saw a shining silver gray.

Trying to better see this thing that looked like shiny smoke
He zoomed in much too quickly and **SMACK** into a mighty oak.

There are some things in life that we will not find when we go and seek
Pursuing unrelated things could be thought a more advisable technique.

Thursday November 21, 2002

The Secretive Stallion

She sauntered into my pasture with her haunches swinging like she just bucked a cowboy. Her mane glistened silver in the sunlight, shinier than a new set of shoes. She had attention written all over her like a fresh cattle brand.

I knew she was trouble when her eye flicked on mine like the whip of an ill-tempered master. It was moments like these that made me regret my coat: too dark a brown to miss in the sunlight, too light a brown to lose in the deepest shadows.

If she thought I'd trot over there like an immature colt eager for his first experience, she had another thing coming. A wild stallion has no master.

I've sired several fine young foals. Dams are a dime a dozen.

brown Wolf

green Eyes

silver Wolf

Thursday November 21, 2002

Metawriting[*]

The experience that changed my life (and therefore shaped me as writer) is love. I am not sure if that actually comes through in these short pieces of writing. To grow and evolve as a person, one needs to try new things, just as a writer needs to try methods and styles of writing to grow and evolve as writer. A silver animal and a brown animal unite my different pieces. My first poem is about a bird who repeatedly does the same thing over and over again, not realizing it is not getting him anywhere until it is too late. He is constantly pursuing love, but he does not stop to think that he does not even know what love really is. I purposefully wrote it in rhyming couplets because that was the only way I would dare writing poetry. I like rhyming poetry; it seems to have more flow, at least in my opinion.

My second piece (short flash fiction) takes the hardboiled detective story to the world of horses for an interesting message: there are lots of fish in the sea (as the old adage goes). Like the bird, however, the stallion has a flawed view of the world. While the bird would try to fall in love with every female he saw, the horse would not care about the females, believing that there are always more. These two creatures are similar to the nice guy and the jerk, respectively (the two categories that most guys in the world fall into). Neither is a completely healthy personality. In between is the great guy.

I debated with myself about whether or not I should have included my third piece, the very short poem about the wolves. I decided to keep it because I should not be tied down by the unnecessary thinking that a poem needs to be a certain length. It conveys what I want to say in six simple words. Wolves are independent, while still being able to share and show affection. The wolf is the great guy of the animal world.

What is the difference between a nice guy, a jerk, and a great guy? Let's say a woman is sitting on the sofa and asks for a glass of water. The nice guy will always be subservient and would jump to get the water, even if he has a broken leg and has to hobble twenty yards to get it while the woman who asked him is perfectly healthy and sitting on the couch. The jerk will never get the woman the glass of water and will always say something the lines of "Bitch, get your own damn water," even if SHE just broke her leg and would have to hobble twenty yards to get it while HE is perfectly healthy and sitting on the couch. The great guy will consider the circumstances first. If he has a broken leg, and the woman is perfectly healthy, he will tell her to get her own glass of water. If, however, she has a broken leg, and he is perfectly healthy, he would be more than glad to get it for her.

---

[*] The previous three pieces were written for a college writing course. This is the explanation I included with them.

"If you want good advice, just listen to your heart. That's the only way to be truly happy in life."

Book of Ley

Sunday November 17, 2002

Dragon Dance

The silver dragon and the brown dragon soared above the clouds, their wings and claws entwined in a loving embrace.

Art in nature. Nature in art. Art as nature. Nature as art. Art = Nature. The beauty of art and nature.

Nature. Sunset. 6:38 PM. October 6, 2002. Fairmount Park. A blanket spread out in the azalea garden behind the Philadelphia Art Museum. After five minutes of wrestling the cap off the sparkling cider bottle with a key, I finally start pouring the bubbly golden liquid into two clear glasses.

Two pieces of jewelry in my bag: a cheap cubic zirconia hanging off an even cheaper bright yellow necklace and a 14 karat yellow gold ring with diamonds totaling 1/6 of a carat, with a special inscription engraved inside: JES LKH CEH – her initials; Love, Kisses, Hugs; my initials. Art.

The necklace was my safety. In case I decided to wait a week. But I already decided earlier in the day that I was going to do it tonight. Better to have her say no than to spend a week charged with nervous energy. Nature.

No set script. No words practiced over and over again in the mirror until they could come almost without thought. My heart spoke for me. The way she makes me feel. Wanting to spend the rest of my life getting to know everything about her. Soul mates. Known her all of eternity and only a fleeting instant.

Art. The ring comes out. The question is asked. Whatever the answer, my life will never be the same. She looks at the ring for a minute then leans over with a passionate kiss.

The brown dragon gently enclosed the silver dragon in his large leathery wings and lightly used his clawed hand to bring the silver dragon's lovely snout closer for a fiery kiss.

The moment we first kissed, I knew she was The One. Something just clicked. Things fit. Like the last two puzzle pieces. With her, life is better. I am myself, but the best version of myself. Opening up a part of me I didn't know was there. A kiss and more than a kiss. Nature.

Cuddled up together on my sofa, snug under a warm comforter. The kiss scene at the end of *The Princess Bride*, a movie we both love. As I bent down to kiss her, I put my finger under her chin to bring her warm lips to mine. "Storybook Love" playing in the background. Perfect. Special. Passionate.

As they shared their fiery kiss, the brown and silver dragons began slowly flapping their lively leathery wings in an almost unconscious movement of ecstasy.

She's kissing me. Dare I hope that means yes? When our lips finally part, I ask. YES!!! In this instant, the world is perfect. She suspected, but hadn't dared hope. I had hinted. Fantasy now. Reality later. Not time for practicalities. My heart's true love. My mind breathes a sigh of relief and allows my heart to have its moment.

Love of my heart. The silkiness of her hair. Her warm brown eyes. Art. Her infectious laughter at the smallest things. The cute little sound she makes with a little jump when I touch her in just the right spot. Soul mate.

My mate. Reaching over. Holding her close. Never let go. This perfect night will never end. Endless embrace. The heat of her body next to mine.

Wrapped in the warm embrace of his heart's true love, the brown dragon's mind absently wandered back to the time he first met the silver dragon, two dragonian weeks ago (roughly equivalent to four millennia in the time of the short-lived humans). He had thought he was the last of the great flying beast when he'd heard the whisperings.

A musician could not play a more melodious tune than the word *yes* coming from my lover's lips. A painter could not paint a more perfect scene than a girl accepting a boy's marriage proposal on a blanket at sunset in the park. Nature and art. Art and nature. Two separate things. One thing.

As Suzi Gablick says, art does not necessarily need to be in a museum or concert hall or theatre to be considered art. The performers do not even need to know that what they are doing is art for it to be considered art. Things naturally and perfectly in harmony with nature can unknowingly be art. One merely needs to spend a few hours in a forest, glade, or other natural setting to see the truth in this statement. The doe quenching her thirst in the mountain stream, the squirrel scurrying up the great oak with an acorn clutched tightly in his grasp, and the mother bear teaching her cubs how to catch fish in the river are all prime examples of art in nature. Even the softest note dropped from the beak of the loneliest bird is art.

The whispering came through the mountains. Soft and sultry it came, calling the brown dragon, urging him to fly high above the clouds, promising him endless joy and boundless pleasure. For what seemed like an eternity, he followed the call, deeper south than he had ever gone before. Over long stretches of empty desolate plains filled with an overwhelming nothing ness and gigantic snow-capped mountains with rocky finger tendrils reaching for the warmth of the sun. Onward he flew, alone and lonely, responding to the mysterious call, knowing in heart only that he must follow it.

In class*, many people agreed "writing is an activity that distances us from others and is often undertaken when feel alienated and alone." Maybe so, but am I writing this because I feel alienated and alone? Actually, it is just the

---

* This piece was also written for a college writing course.

opposite. I am writing this paper because I am more in touch and aligned with another person than I have ever been before in my entire life. Does writing this distance me from other people. Not at all. In fact, I believe it will actually make me closer to the most important person in my life. It is a way to preserve the memory of a most important event in our two lives. I get a warm feeling thinking about her reading my heart's words put on paper. Another silk thread woven into the connection between our souls.

Something silver in the distance reflecting the golden light of the sun. The brown dragon begins to beat his leathery wings faster, his large heart pounding in his chest. Could it possibly be? Another dragon? He could scarcely believe his eyes — the last living female of his species. It was her melodious call he had been following. His heart ten times larger, he approaches her, and their talons and wings naturally and artfully intertwine.

Dragon Dance

The silver dragon and the brown dragon soared above the clouds, their wings and claws entwined in a loving embrace.

The brown dragon gently enclosed the silver dragon in his large leathery wings and lightly used his clawed hand to bring the silver dragon's lovely snout closer for a fiery kiss.

As they shared their fiery kiss, the brown and silver dragons began slowly flapping their lively leathery wings in an almost unconscious movement of ecstasy.

Wrapped in the warm embrace of his heart's true love, the brown dragon's mind absently wandered back to the time he first met the silver dragon, two dragonian weeks ago (roughly equivalent to four millennia in the time of the short-lived humans). He had thought he was the last of the great flying beast when he'd heard the whisperings.

The whispering came through the mountains. Soft and sultry it came, calling the brown dragon, urging him to fly high above the clouds, promising him endless joy and boundless pleasure. For what seemed like an eternity, he followed the call, deeper south than he had ever gone before. Over long stretches of empty desolate plains filled with an overwhelming nothing ness and gigantic snow-capped mountains with rocky finger tendrils reaching for the warmth of the sun. Onward he flew, alone and lonely, responding to the mysterious call, knowing in heart only that he must follow it.

Something silver in the distance reflecting the golden light of the sun. The brown dragon begins to beat his leathery wings faster, his large heart pounding in his chest. Could it possibly be? Another dragon? He could scarcely believe his eyes — the last living female of his species. It was her melodious call he had been following. His heart ten times larger, he approaches her, and their talons and wings naturally and artfully intertwine.

Monday March 6, 2002

Seaching for Soul Mates[*]

"One's perceived soul mate is often the conglomeration of one's former lovers combined with one's dream of the ideal woman" (William[**]). To discuss a concept with people, one must first know how those people define that particular concept. Since the topic of this project is soul mates, it is necessary to know how people define the phrase "soul mates". Although definitions of soul mate(s) vary from "people who are basically meant for each other" (Paul) to "a person you can imagine yourself growing old with" (Mary), the one thing that all the definitions seem to agree with is that the concept of soul mates involves two people who are meant to be together.

For as long as I can remember, I have been interested in the concept of true love, and I believe that there is one woman out there who is meant for me, just as I am meant for her. This is probably why my favorite movie is *The Princess Bride*, a bent fairy tale, which, in spite of its fictional nature, I feel is a real portrayal of true love. Neither the hero nor the heroine understand the other fully and, at times, confuse one another.

Do college students (specifically Drexel University students living on the seventh floor of Calhoun Hall) believe in soul mates, and, if so, 1) why do these students believe in the concept of soul mates and 2) what are these students looking for in a soul mate? I am very interested in the subject of soul mates and am curious as to how other Drexel students are searching for their soul mates, as well as what they look for in their soul mates, or even if they believe in soul mates.

I conducted my research on the seventh floor of Calhoun Hall, a dormitory for Drexel University freshman and transfer students. Calhoun Hall is an eight-story building located on Arch Street between 33rd Street and 34th Street. The seventh floor is evenly divided between men and women, with approximately 25 men (including me) on one wing of the floor and the same number of women on the other wing of the floor. Other than the fact that all the students living on the seventh floor of Calhoun Hall are either freshmen or transfer students at Drexel, it is a fairly random sample of new Drexel students, with an even amount of men and women ranging in age from eighteen years old to twenty-five years old.

In order to obtain the information I needed, I designed a survey containing general questions on the topic of soul mates, with the intention of

---

[*] Adapted from a project paper for a college course.

[**] Due to the personal and confidential nature of this topic, all the names of the people talked to have been changed.

eliciting detailed information from the respondents upon the return of the survey. I went around the floor on the evening of Tuesday, February 12, 2002, to distribute the surveys. I managed to speak to about ten people personally about the survey and this project and slipped the remaining forty copies of the survey under doors for the people who were not available. I encouraged people to fill out the survey and provide me with information by offering a free mystery gift (a handmade bookmark with hearts and a ribbon) upon the return of the survey. I also gave people four days to fill out the survey, so they could do it at their convenience.

By Friday, February 15, 2002 (the due date of the survey), I had received back a total of fifteen surveys (including those filled out by myself and my roommate). Considering there are fifty people on my floor, this was not a bad response rate. The fifteen people were almost even split between genders, with eight women and seven men. After reviewing the survey answers and conducting detailed interviews with the respondents, it quickly became obvious who my key informants were: Susan and Paul. From these two people, I easily got the most detailed and relevant information about the topic of soul mates.

I used the self-reflexivity approach[1] when conducting my research. Not only did I realize my own bias in order to take a more objective view, but also I was also able to use my bias as an advantage when I designed the survey and interview questions. My bias was that I thought most people believed in the concept of soul mates. All fifteen respondents said that they believe in the concept of soul mates. Was the fact that the survey was about a concept they believed in make them more likely to fill it out and talk with me? I believe it was, and I even anticipated this. Because everyone I talked to about this project believed in the concept of soul mates, I was able to get more detailed information about the topic, although it only applies to a smaller portion of the people on the floor. Had most of the people who responded to the survey professed to not believing in the concept of soul mates, the results of my research, while being more accurate as to how many people believe in the soul mates, would have been completely useless.

Instead of being useless, my research led me to uncover some rather fascinating things. One discovery I made is that, while height did not matter to about half of the participants, all the men preferred a woman who was their height or shorter, and all the women preferred a man who was their height or taller. There were several characteristics that almost everyone included as one of the five most important for their soul mates to possess: honesty, kindness, loyalty, and intelligence. All these things can be considered to be positive characteristics or traits, and none of the participants in my research would want a soul mate extremely lacking in one or more of these areas.

---

[1] Tran, Hoa. Class Lecture. Anth 101-002. Drexel University. January 7, 2002.

Even though almost all of my informants are dating, only two have boyfriends or girlfriends and none are in serious relationships. All of the informants believe that it is extremely unlikely they will find their soul mates while they are still in college and that they probably will not find their soul mates for several years after that.

Like Tylor's concept of animism[2] (the belief in the existence of spirits), the belief in soul mates is a belief of faith. One can argue against the existence of soul mates as easily as one can argue for the existence of soul mates; one needs faith to believe that soul mates exist. This is clearly evident from the survey responses and interview answers: "[Soul mates] are two people who just 'click' from the start. When they are around each other, magic happens" (Kelly); "[A soul mate] is someone whom you were destined to spend your life with" (Rose); "[Your soul mate] is someone you could spend all eternity with" (Paul); "[Your soul mate] is the person G-d separated you from before birth" (Deborah). All these statements require a large degree of faith.

When asked why they believe in soul mates, almost all my informants gave answers that lacked logical reasoning. Jennifer simply believes that "eventually everyone will meet someone who they are supposed to spend their life with." Mary just stated, "Everyone has that special someone out there." Only two people gave reasons with some logical backing. James observed that there are "married couples who have been so happy over the years." Paul reasoned, "There is someone for everyone because there are all types of people who could match your interests and personality." The most faith-based answer came from a Jewish female, Susan, who told me about the Jewish belief in soul mates:

> In Judaism there is a concept of a soul mate . . . we call them *bashert*. It is said in the oral Torah that a person is given a *bashert* 40 days before they are born. Also, it is said that when we are married, that is when we complete our souls.

Obviously, to believe in the existence of soul mates, one has to have faith.

Another thing that contributes to the belief in a soul mate is one's personal culture[3], a concept discussed in class. The society and environment in which people are raised play a large factor in determining what concepts they will or will not believe in. Emile Durkheim, the French social scientist, believed in the existence of the *conscience collective*[4], a French phrase which can be best translated into English as "shared awareness" or "common understanding." In

---

[2] Tylor, Edward Burnett. In High Points in Anthropology, edited by Paul Bohannan and Mark Glazer. Second Edition. New York: McGraw-Hill, Inc. 1988.

[3] Tran, Hoa. Class Lecture. Anth 101-002. Drexel University. January 7, 2002.

[4] Durkheim, Emile. In High Points in Anthropology, edited by Paul Bohannan and Mark Glazer. Second Edition. New York: McGraw-Hill, Inc. 1988.

our society, the existence of soul mates is a widely held belief and can be seen in popular culture, from the cult classic *The Princess Bride* to the romantic comedy *When Harry Met Sally* to the recent drama *Dragonfly*. One can clearly see that the concept of soul mates is a firmly ingrained part of our *conscience collective*.

According to Michel Foucault[5], the French philosopher, "Knowledge is power." How does this apply to the concept of soul mates? If one were to take the phrase literally, one would think Foucault means that the more knowledge a person has of what he/she is looking for in soul mate, as well as how and where he/she can find it, the more power a person has when looking for his/her soul mate. Thus, the more knowledge a person has about his/her soul mate, the easier it is for him/her to find his/her soul mate. Looking closer at what Foucault has to say about this simple phrase, one can see that this is not quite what he has in mind. Foucault was "interested in [the] knowledge *of* human beings and [the] power that acts *on* human beings." Mainly, he was interested in how physical and mental forces can be exerted by a powerful minority to impose their idea of what is right on the majority. Is a minority of the population using mental force to impose the belief in the existence of soul mates on the majority? If they are, I can conceive of no reasonable explanation of why they would do this. Therefore, although on first glance Foucault's phrase "knowledge is power" seems to be closely related to the concept of soul mates, on closer examination, what he was saying really has little to do with soul mates. If one just takes the phrase literally and does not delve more deeply into what Foucault was saying, the simple phrase "knowledge is power" becomes deeply entwined with the concept of soul mates.

The concept of soul mates can be explored in many ways, and although this research has been mainly of use to myself, many people would be interested to know more about the topic of soul mates. In our society, the concept of soul mates has become an increasingly frequent topic of discussion. The British philosopher Jeremy Bentham said that mankind has two masters: pleasure and pain[6]. The main goal of mankind is to seek pleasure and avoid pain. Having a soul mate would produce a great deal of pleasure for many people and is only one of the many things that people are looking for to give them pleasure. A soul mate can provide one with a great deal of happiness and fulfillment.

---

[5] Fillingham, Lydia Alix. Foucault for Beginners. New York, NY: Writers and Readers Publishing, Inc. 1993. Pp. 5-18.

[6] Bentham, Jeremy. The Principles of Morals and Legislation. Amherst, NY: Prometheus Books. 1988. Originally published in 1781.

"The man who has everything has nothing to strive for."

Book of Ley

Author's Note

Names and certain identifying features have been changed for privacy reasons. Other than that, everything in here is true and happened to me. It was fitting that I finished this book as my first quarter century of life drew to a close. Writing this book allowed me to bring closure to a section of my life and putting it all down here lifted a huge weight off; it allowed me to finally let go. Yes, I have loved and lost. More than once. And I'm sure it'll happen again. Probably several more times before I eventually find the right woman for me. Life isn't a race or a competition, and I can be happy with what I have.

I hope my story encourages other people dealing with overwhelming issues to seek help before doing anything extreme. I was lucky; I almost chose a permanent solution to some temporary problems. Things can and do get better. Depression and mental illness is more common than you think. Even with a background in psychology and counseling, I still felt stigmatized by having a "mental illness" and needing medication. I was pleasantly surprised by the overwhelming support I received. Of everyone I talked to about my depression, the only person who thought I "should pull myself up by the bootstraps" was myself. To some extent I still feel that way, but I always know help is available.

If you feel like you're having difficulty handling life, I want you to know that help is out there, and there are people who care about you. If you're a college student, go to your counseling center. If not, there are many resources available. Even if you feel that no one cares what happens to you, know that there is one person who does: me.

Thank you for taking the time to read my book, and I wish you all the good things life has to offer.

C

June 10, 2007

About the Author

C. E. Haas lives in NJ. He works with kids and plays with books. He enjoys lifting weights and occasionally picking up women.

_____

www.ingramcontent.com/pod-product-compliance
Lightning Source LLC
LaVergne TN
LVHW091152080426
835509LV00006B/646